# The
# SANCTUARY
## *for Lent*
## 2008

ISBN 978-0-687-64148-2
ISSN 0270-1758

Scripture quotations unless otherwise marked are from the *Revised Standard Version of the Bible,* copyright 1946, 1952, 1971 by the Division of Christian Education of the National Council of the Churches of Christ in the United States of America. Used by permission. All rights reserved.

Scripture quotations marked (NIV) are taken from the HOLY BIBLE, NEW INTERNATIONAL VERSION®. NIV®. Copyright © 1973, 1978, 1984 by International Bible Society. Used by permission of Zondervan Publishing House. All rights reserved.

*Fasting*

*Read Matthew 6:16-18*

**When you fast, anoint your head and wash your face, that your fasting may not be seen by men but by your Father who is in secret.**
— *(Matthew 6:17-18)*

Nothing is more alien to our culture than fasting. But Moses, Jesus, and saints through history knew the importance of fasting.

Fasting isn't giving up something harmful; fasting is giving up something good, which I do without for a time for the sake of God. When we satisfy every desire, our deeper desire for God is numbed. I fast to recover a deeper quest than the satisfaction of my desires. I blunt those desires to whet my appetite for God.

When hunger gnaws, I discover how hollow I am, how superficial I can be. We also learn a solidarity with the needy and are drawn to understand and care for them.

Francis of Assisi once fasted for forty days, but on the thirty-ninth day he broke the fast, as he might be tempted to think he was as holy as Jesus. This Lent, we will listen to the teachings of Jesus—the bread of life, which alone satisfies our hunger.

*Prayer:* Lord, teach me the discipline of fasting in Lent; I want to hunger only for you.

## Blessed

*Read Matthew 5:1-8*

*[Jesus] opened his mouth and taught them, saying: "Blessed are the poor in spirit, for theirs is the kingdom of heaven.*      *—Matthew 5:2-3*

On a lovely hill, Jesus spoke to people who were poor, meek, overtaxed, hungry—nobodies really, eager for God to intervene and improve their lot.

In a way Jesus is recommending what we need to cultivate in our hearts: a poverty of spirit aware of its need for God, a humble meekness, a pure heart, mercy, a hunger for intimacy with God. In another sense, these "beatitudes" are autobiographical: Jesus was poor; he mourned not just death but also how the world gets out of sync with God. He was meek. His food was doing God's will. He was merciful with the worst people. His heart was pure . . . So the closer we get to Jesus, the more these "beatitudes" describe us.

Jesus offers us a place in the kingdom of God, comfort when there is no comfort, righteousness, mercy, and a reasonably clear glimpse of God—which is plenty enough, right?

*Prayer:* Lord, help me begin to discover in my soul a hunger for righteousness, and to expect your blessings of mercy and comfort.

*Pacifists and Persecution*

*Read Matthew 5:9-12*

**Blessed are the peacemakers, for they shall be called sons of God. Blessed are those who are persecuted for righteousness' sake.**

—*Matthew 5:9-10*

Jesus promises not just marvelous blessings, but more darkly, the pledge that sticking close to him will put you at odds with people who will hurt you. How did he expect to attract a following with such bleak prospects?

Throughout history, Jesus' followers have been despised, lost jobs, been executed—but have found immense joy in it all, the delight of being swept up in the adventure of Jesus.

These days, you will be ridiculed if you push for peace. In politics, TV, and personal life, our society resorts to force to settle conflict. But Jesus said, "Blessed are the peacemakers." Peacemakers *make* peace. They are not passive; they do something; they engage the other and never tire of laboring for reconciliation. Jesus (the Prince of peace) made peace, and so we never flag in our zeal to pray and diligently strive for peace—in the world, the community, our homes, and our hearts.

*Prayer:* Lord, make me an instrument of your peace.

## *"I'm Gonna Let It Shine"*

*Read Matthew 5:13-20*

***You are the salt of the earth. . . .You are the light of the world.*** —*Matthew 5:13-14*

You are salt. Salt preserves, purifies, seasons—and we have the privilege as God's people to be salt: we bring out the best, we protect and prolong life, and we have a subtle cleansing effect on the world. In Bible times, salt was a metaphor for wisdom—and salt was used in the Temple sacrifices. You are salt: be wise.

You are the light of the world. America's colonists felt they were to be this light to the nations. The church is to be a lighthouse bringing lost ships home in the night. "This little light of mine, I'm gonna let it shine"— isn't smiling sweetly, but living in an exemplary way that refracts like a prism the light of God's grace—but not in a smug way.

During a baptism, many churches light a candle, symbolic of Jesus, "the light of the world," and say "Let your light so shine before [others], that they may see your good works and give glory to your Father who is in heaven."

*Prayer:* Lord, I will be your salt and your light. Even a small, flickering candle banishes darkness from a room.

## Anger and Adultery

*Read Matthew 5:21-37*

**But I say to you that every one who looks at a woman lustfully has already committed adultery with her in his heart.** —Matthew 5:28

Many Christians want to toss the Old Testament out. But Jesus treasured it and taught us to observe not merely its letter, but its deeper spirit. To all who think they revere the Ten Commandments, Jesus makes us tremble by cutting to the marrow of God's intent.

Never killed? Good—but Jesus says if you harbor anger in your mind, you are guilty of murder. How strange! Isn't it delicious to vent, find fault, get mad? But anger isn't just a sword pointed at somebody else; it lacerates me and alienates me from Jesus.

*Adultery:* a word fallen out of usage. Today, an "affair" is excused for trifling reasons. But how devastating is adultery? Lust, the linchpin of advertising, the plot of so many shows, treats another person as an object, as a thing to be used for my pleasure, not as a child of God. My inner thoughts matter; they ruin me, or they become the mind of Christ in me.

*Prayer:* Lord, I confess my anger, my murderous guilt, and my lust, my disordered desire. Forgive and heal me.

## Love Your Enemies

*Read Matthew 5:38-48*

**But I say to you, Love your enemies and pray for those who persecute you.** —*Matthew 5:44*

We live in a society that insists on "rights," on people getting what they deserve, where revenge seems fair. So how vast is the canyon separating us from Jesus, who not only *said* "Love your enemies," but actually loved them?

Who is my enemy? Someone who hurt me? Someone who's different, who threatens me? Followers of Jesus do not even the score; they shrink back from retaliation in any form. Followers of Jesus know that "love bears all things" (1 Corinthians 13:7), and we expect that we will suffer disadvantage because of our Christlike posture in the face of hatred.

Isn't it unthinkable not to resist? But our standard is Jesus, whose mission was to reconcile us who have become enemies of God and each other, who made forgiveness reality, who was rejected by those he loved, who was innocent but was executed.

There is only one way to get rid of an enemy: to love, to befriend that enemy who then is no longer an enemy.

*Prayer:* Lord, help me identify my enemies and then love them.

*Alms*

*Read Matthew 6:1-4*

**When you give alms, sound no trumpet before you, as the hypocrites do.** —*Matthew 6:2*

"When you give alms, sound no trumpet"? In Bible times, "sophar chests" were set up in the Temple—trumpet-shaped receptacles that resounded when coins were dropped in, calling attention to the giver.

No danger of trumpets blaring nowadays. It's impolite for church people to talk about money; we practice anonymous giving. But doesn't anonymous giving easily become anonymous nongiving? While spiritual humility insists we not flaunt our giving, most of us should be embarrassed by how little we give.

Your heavenly Father, who sees what you give in secret, will ask for some reckoning when the trumpet sounds at the end of time. What did you do, not with 10 percent or whatever money you had left over after necessities, mortgages, hobbies, and diversions—but what did you do with *all* of it?

*Prayer:* Lord, I blush when I remember you know how little I give. I promise you a revolution in my giving—a secret from others but not from you.

## The Lord's Prayer

*Read Matthew 6:5-15*

**When you pray, you must not be like the hypocrites.** —*Matthew 6:5*

"When you pray"—not *if* you pray! Assuming we would pray often, he offered a memorable, simple model of how to talk with God.

We address God not as a remote potentate, but as Father, "Abba," an intimate term children young and old used for their dad. God is "our" Father; we join hands with others.

Jesus' prayer is not just "Help me, give me . . ." Its first movement is to extol the greatness of God. We seek "thy kingdom come." And how profound is the prayer for forgiveness if all hinges on how merciful we are to others?

A wise way to use the Lord's Prayer is to pause and personalize each sentence. "Forgive us our trespasses—such as . . ." "As we forgive those—such as . . ." "Lead us not into temptation—especially . . ."

*Prayer:* "Our Father, who art in heaven, Hallowed be thy name. Thy kingdom come, Thy will be done on earth as in heaven. Give us our daily bread, and forgive us our debts, As we also have forgiven our debtors; And lead us not into temptation, But deliver us from evil."

9

## Treasure in Heaven

*Read Matthew 6:19-34*

**Do not lay up for yourselves treasures on earth . . .
but lay up for yourselves treasures in heaven.**
**—Matthew 6:19-20**

Ever notice that the financial industry uses religious terminology? *Trust, security, faith, debt, fidelity, future, equity, save* . . . Is money our true religion? Isn't treasure on earth what life is about—to invest, purchase, own? We don't worry about moth, rust, or thieves; we've got insurance.

God wired the human heart in an unexpected, upside-down, and merciful way. Spend yourself investing in stuff, and you wind up with a heart that is hollow, mean, or trivial. Do you see the world and your life through Jesus' eyes?

Real treasure (being driven by Jesus, giving everything to him) yields a heart that is full, kind, and calm. Money and things seem to block us from a good heart, don't they? "Empty hands reach out for God; full hands are clutched to the self" (Dale Allison).

*Prayer:* Lord, I've laid up treasure on earth for too long; I shove that away now and begin investing myself in treasure in heaven.

## *Log in the Eye*

*Read Matthew 7:1-6*

***Why do you see the speck that is in your brother's eye, but do not notice the log that is in your own eye?*** *—Matthew 7:3*

The crowd probably chuckled when Jesus tossed out the ludicrous image of somebody trying to get a splinter out of another person's eye—with a whole tree trunk stuck in his own! But it is not very funny if we admit to our dreadful habit of faultfinding.

Jesus isn't saying we should avoid thinking diligently about right and wrong. But if you have the energy of a lumberjack, spend it on the log in yourself. Why find splinters in others? Aren't we insecure, hoping to inflate our own puny egos? The soul intimately in sync with Jesus notices nothing but good. "Whatever is pure, whatever is lovely, . . . if there is any excellence, if there is anything worthy of praise, think about these things" (Philippians 4:8).

Jesus has freed me from judging my neighbor. I am incapable of it anyhow, but the responsibility isn't mine even if I were capable.

*Prayer:* Lord, I am addicted to finding fault. Work with me on the log in my own eye. I leave the judging to you.

## *Does Prayer Work?*

*Read Matthew 7:7-23*

***Ask, and it will be given you; seek, and you will find; knock, and it will be opened to you.***
***—Matthew 7:7***

Does prayer work? When Jesus says, "Ask, and it will be given," he isn't saying prayer is a machine. Prayer is love. Prayer is a relationship. How do fathers love their children? Not by simply doling out whatever the child wants. The wisest gift is restraint. The most tender gift is trusting the child to stand or fall on his own. Children know no better than to ask for stones and serpents (or their modern equivalents). But good fathers give bread and fish.

And aren't bread and fish ancient symbols of the presence of Christ? What better gift can a father give a child than his own self, his time, his love? What better gift could God give us than God's own self in Jesus? Ask, and you will receive. God gives the most precious gift: his own Son—and whatever else he finds to be genuinely helpful to your soul.

*Prayer:* Lord, I am knocking. Help me to want what you want. Give me only the finest of all conceivable gifts: your self.

12

## Building a House

*Read Matthew 7:24-29*

**A wise man . . . built his house upon the rock.**
*—Matthew 7:24*

What is the goal of life? We want "to be happy." Often we measure happiness by whether we are having "fun" or not. But what if we got up in the morning and said "What can we do so we can be faithful today? or good? Is what we are doing helping us or our children become wise or holy?"

"Unless the Lord builds the house, those who build it labor in vain" (Psalm 127:1). Jesus concludes his masterful sermon with a metaphor from construction—and as an apprentice carpenter, Jesus knew building.

What kind of life have you constructed? What is its foundation? its materials? its use? In deciding what checks to write, what to stick on your calendar, what you have avoided, shows you've watched, words you've said, all your activities, have you lived out Joshua's pledge? "As for me and my house, we will serve the LORD" (Joshua 24:15).

*Prayer:* Lord, my house is in disarray. Do not merely spruce it up a bit. Demolish its flimsy foundations and rebuild my house based on your will.

## The Call of Matthew

*Read Matthew 9:9-13*

**"Why does your teacher eat with tax collectors and sinners?"**          **—Matthew 9:11**

In Capernaum, if you said "tax collector," you paused to spit in disgust. Tax collectors were the unethical henchmen of an evil empire, forcibly overcharging the poor to line their own pockets while funding Rome's wars and buildings. For Jesus even to speak to such a hated person as Matthew was scandalous.

Jesus not only welcomes him into his movement, he makes him a disciple, one of his inner circle. But Jesus isn't trying to please anybody; he isn't guarding against criticism. He is the vanguard of a new world, where everyone finds a home, where both the horrifically behaved and the smugly pious are on the same footing.

How do Jesus' followers adjust? How does Matthew adjust? Imagine giving up a profitable life to hang with the people who've spat at you? What about us? Who is despised? Somebody out there I need to include? Somebody inside me I haven't acknowledged? Who needs a physician?

*Prayer:* Lord, I am sick, needing you, the great Physician. Help me see every other person as a patient on whom you have immense compassion.

## *Harvest Plentiful, Laborers Few*

*Read Matthew 9:35-38*

**When [Jesus] saw the crowds, he had compassion.**
**—Matthew 9:36**

Jesus had compassion. But why? They were not spiritual soldiers, marching in holy array. They were "harassed and helpless." How do we look at crowds, at the throng out there in the world? We may not notice them, or we may formulate criticism in our minds for why these people are what's wrong with the world.

If we see with Jesus' eyes, we notice that people are harassed and helpless. People feel mistreated, victims of large forces that hamper development. Their very efforts to help themselves are misguided; without God they are stuck being harassed and helpless. They need the attention of God's people.

Can we feel for them what Jesus felt? Can we enlist as one of the laborers for the harvest for which Jesus prayed? What can I do to ensure the bumper crop of human potential doesn't rot out in the field?

*Prayer:* Lord, help me see with Jesus' compassion; sign me up as a worker in your ripe fields.

## A Cup of Water

*Read Matthew 10:40-42*

**Whoever gives to one of these little ones even a cup of cold water . . . shall not lose his reward.**
—Matthew 10:42

Thérèse of Lisieux enjoyed a remarkably intimate relationship with Jesus. She focused on seemingly trivial, small acts of love. She called it "the little way"—for simple deeds of love are the life of holiness; God's power is revealed in our weakness.

Jesus, preparing his followers for opposition they inevitably would face, kept it simple. If God cares for sparrows, virtual nothings, then how much more does God care for you?

The Christian life can seem ominous, a Grand Canyon of impossibly deep thought and challenge. But it all comes down to a cup of water, something little, a tender act of love offered in Christ's name.

*Prayer:* Lord, help me prepare for the difficulties of following you; remind me to keep it simple, to focus on the insignificant, which is all that is significant in the end. Teach me "the little way."

### *Hidden Revealed*

*Read Matthew 11:25-27*

**[You have] hidden these things from the wise and understanding and revealed them to babes.**
**—*Matthew 11:25***

Poke around behind rocks, analyze mountains of facts—but you will not find God. We only know God because God reveals God to us. Children, under no illusion they know it all, get it, while the clever miss out (1 Corinthians 1:18-31).

We can never fathom the majestically incomprehensible fullness of God. If the brain could master God, God would not be God. God wants a childlike humility, so God always acts contrary to what we expect. God hides his power in weakness. Mary was lowly; there was no room at the inn.

Jesus entered Jerusalem, not on a war stallion but on a wretched donkey. Instead of crushing his foes, he was crucified. When God seems absent, when all is darkness, in the middle of suffering, then God is genuinely present, embracing our mortality and suffering.

*Prayer:* I thank you that you have hidden these things from the wise and understanding and revealed them to infants.

## Take My Yoke

*Read Matthew 11:28-30*

**Come to me, all who labor and are heavy laden, and I will give you rest.        —*Matthew 11:28***

When people in counseling are asked, "What one adjective describes how you feel?" the top answer is "Tired." We feel like Atlas, weary from trying to carry the whole world on our shoulders.

"Come to me . . . I will give you rest." Connecting with Jesus isn't piling extra poundage on the schedule. We can lay a lot of other things down; "He's got the whole world in his hands," so we don't have to tote it any longer.

Jesus isn't saying his "yoke" is easy or undemanding. But when our most zealous efforts are expended on something that matters, something true and going somewhere, we don't flag with exhaustion.

And we can rest. God made provision for a merciful day of rest—and we *can* rest, since it isn't all up to me and my feverish activity. We can rest in love and grace; the Lord of the universe is "gentle," lifting us up and bringing us home.

*Prayer:* Lord, I am coming to you heavy laden. Give me rest. I willingly take your yoke.

## Sabbath

*Read Matthew 12:1-14*

***I desire mercy, and not sacrifice. —Matthew 12:7***

For Jews, the Sabbath mattered. God wired us, taking into account our need for Sabbath: a day of reflection, rest, focused devotion to God—a day of equality. We've ruined the Sabbath by our secular lifestyle preferences, our frenetic pace. Time is never sacred. Little wonder we are so stressed and fatigued.

Jesus, of all people, was upbraided for failure to observe the Sabbath. But he didn't open his carpentry shop or catch up on shopping. He let the hungry eat; he healed a man. His critics, so adamant about God's will, misconstrued the heart of the Sabbath. Jesus' Father "desire[s] mercy, not sacrifice" (Hosea 6:6 NIV). The Sabbath is not a harsh demand. The Sabbath is mercy: we need rest, worship, a day to remember it's in God's hands.

To Jesus Sabbath was sacred—so sacred you couldn't let the hungry languish or let suffering linger. If we do anything other than rest on the Sabbath, does it qualify as mercy? feeding the hungry? healing those in agony?

*Prayer:* Lord, I will rethink observing the Sabbath; I need a day to discover your mercy.

SUNDAY, FEBRUARY 24, 2008

*The Unforgivable Sin*

Read Matthew 12:31-32

***Every sin and blasphemy will be forgiven.***
***—Matthew 12:31***

"The passages in Scripture which trouble me most are those I *do* understand" (Mark Twain). But with this strangest of Jesus' thoughts, the probing Bible reader worries about what we *don't* understand. We need to weigh the context. The Pharisees have just accused Jesus of being in league with the devil; his healing power is demonic, not divine. So Jesus rages in reply, declaring that the worst sin is to twist God's saving purpose and attribute it to the devil.

How broad is forgiveness, if only this is unforgivable! If we fail to understand exactly what Jesus meant, we're forgiven. And if you *are* worried about having committed the unforgivable sin, you can hardly be guilty of it.

*Prayer:* Lord, help me be careful how I talk about you, and the Spirit. I would never pair you with the devil. I would never reject your precious forgiveness.

*Jesus' Brothers and Sisters*
Read Matthew 12:46-50

**Who is my mother, and who are my brothers?**
**—Matthew 12:48**

Who was in Jesus' family? Matthew 13:55 names at least six siblings! Jesus' answer is striking. His family came to hear him. Instead of having them ushered to seats of honor, Jesus dismissed their importance: Whoever does God's will is Jesus' mother, brother, sister. Earlier he had said, "I have come to set a man against his father, and a daughter against her mother" (Matthew 10:35).

Jesus tells the truth: the demands of God's kingdom can divide people. Jesus isn't a prop to shore up family life or the glue of family values. Jesus' call is radical—and he invites us into a new family, a new fellowship of belonging even deeper and more enduring than blood relations.

St. Francis gave his father's wealth to the poor—and found himself jailed, then sued by his father. He announced publicly, from now on I will say: 'Our Father who art in Heaven' instead of 'my father Pietro Bernardone.'"

*Prayer:* Lord, you are my Father; we who follow you are your true family.

## A Sower Went out to Sow

*Read Matthew 13:1-9*

**A sower went out to sow.**            —*Matthew 13:3*

A familiar sight: a sower laboring. Perhaps Jesus noticed one on the hillside as he spoke. But the sower in this parable seems careless, flinging the seed any and everywhere.

We may ask, "What kind of soil am I?" Am I fertile, ready for the gospel to flourish in me? or am I thorny soil, an unlikely place for the gospel to take root? The first Christians understood Jesus' picturesque image: sometimes their evangelizing blossomed beautifully, but more often it seemed to die out quickly; opponents pecked away at whatever chance there was of success.

But might Jesus be portraying God? This sower is indiscriminate: he doesn't just look for rich soil. He flings it everywhere, on all types. Farmers know that seed sometimes spills, and you wind up with "volunteer" vegetables in uncultivated spots: the seed bears within itself the potential for life in even unexpected places—as does the gospel (Isaiah 55:10-11).

*Prayer:* Lord, we praise you for being a Sower who flings grace on everybody.

## The Secrets of the Kingdom

*Read Matthew 13:10-17*

***Why do you speak to them in parables?***
***—Matthew 13:10***

Remember high school math? A parabola curves elegantly around a focal point, equidistant to a line, never touching the line or the focal point. Like Aristotle or Plato, Jesus tells "parables," stories that curl us toward the focus of our lives, the kingdom of God. Clarence Jordan said that a parable of Jesus is like a Trojan horse: you let it in, and then— Bam!—it's got you.

Jesus didn't teach by listing bullet points, propositions to be believed. Instead, he told stories about farmers, fishermen, parents, bridesmaids. Why? Stories are memorable.

More elusively, Jesus explained that he taught with stories in order to hide and reveal—all at the same time! Whether we "get" the story, whether the parable "works" or not, depends on our inner, spiritual posture.

*Prayer:* Lord, thank you for Jesus' parables; I want my life's story illumined by Jesus' stories.

## Pearl

*Read Matthew 13:44-46*

**The kingdom of heaven is like treasure hidden in a field.** *—Matthew 13:44*

How is the kingdom like someone sprinting away from discovered treasure, selling everything to possess it—or a jewel merchant finding the world's most extraordinary pearl and without a second thought selling everything to have it? The gospel is fabulous treasure, the priceless pearl. It is not fairly valuable, or somewhat worthwhile. It is everything; all else pales by comparison.

Dietrich Bonhoeffer explained "the cost of discipleship." You shed other securities, release well-devised plans. "Cheap grace is forgiveness without repentance . . . grace without discipleship, grace without the cross, grace without Jesus Christ. Costly grace is the treasure hidden in the field; for the sake of it, a man will gladly sell all he has. It is the pearl of great price . . . Grace is *costly* because it calls us to follow, and it is *grace* because it calls us to follow Jesus Christ. . . . Above all, it is costly because it cost God the life of his Son."

*Prayer:* Lord, I want to pursue you, the treasure, the pearl, with total abandon.

## Peter, the Rock

*Read Matthew 16:18*

**On this rock I will build my church.**
                                    *—Matthew 16:18*

Jesus devised a pun that works in two languages! Peter is to be *petros* (Greek for "rock"); Cephas (Peter's Aramaic name) is to be *cepha* (Aramaic for "rock"). "On you, Rock, I will build my church." Did Jesus found a church? Wasn't he instigating a movement, which the church has messed up?

Many spiritual people today feel the church is no longer helpful, and actually gets in the way of relating to God. The church can be an embarrassment to itself and to God.

Perhaps Jesus should have found a more qualified, noble candidate than Peter—and perhaps Jesus should find better people than us today. But the church doesn't depend on the brains and brilliance of its members or leaders. The church is of God.

Don't we need each other to follow Jesus? How lonely to go it alone! We need friends. Friends care about the truth. Friends help each other to love God.

*Prayer:* Lord, thank you for the church, foibles and all. Use us to help each other follow you.

## The Keys of the Kingdom

*Read Matthew 16:19-20*

**I will give you the keys of the kingdom of heaven.**
—*Matthew 16:19*

Why do we need the church? Jesus' movement was designed to transform the world. It's hard to do that on your own! But together we can do amazing things: missions, building, worship, service, programming, advocacy.

In church, you have to deal with people you wouldn't otherwise deal with. But that was the jolt the first Christians delivered to society: rich, poor, Jew, Greek, holy, despised, all suddenly were joined in a single fellowship, a deep family. There had to be friction! But friction can start a fire; friction polishes.

Jesus uses the image of "keys." Keys open doors and let people in; keys secure what is good and protect what's precious. The church has an immense responsibility: what we do has eternal implications. We are not a nice place where nice people do nice things with other nice people. Salvation and the future of the world are at stake!

*Prayer:* Lord, the keys to your kingdom are in our hands. We will use them faithfully for your kingdom.

### Take Up Your Cross

Read Matthew 16:20-28

**Jesus began to show his disciples that he must go to Jerusalem and suffer many things.**
— **Matthew 16:21**

Jesus is the Christ, active, powerful. But now he turns to Jerusalem; instead of acting powerfully, he will be acted upon. He will suffer.

Jesus says "Take up your cross." Aleksandr Solzhenitsyn, condemned to the gulag under Stalin, wrote, "From the moment you go to prison you must put your cozy past firmly behind you. At the threshold, you must say to yourself: 'My former life is over, I shall never return. I no longer have property. Only my spirit and my conscience remain precious to me.'" To follow Jesus, we leave an old, cozy life behind. We learn self-denial, which paradoxically is the only true self-fulfillment.

Notice that the way to be the church is tied to the way Jesus was the Messiah! It's not about success or big numbers, but humbly suffering, renouncing all security, becoming vulnerable, totally obedient to God.

*Prayer:* Lord, I leave my cozy past behind. I deny my self. My richest gain I count but loss for the chance to be near you.

*Become like Children*

Read Matthew 18:1-4

**Unless you turn and become like children, you will never enter the kingdom.**
                                    —*Matthew 18:3*

Typically we attach warm adjectives to this idea of being childlike: we say children are honest, pure, loving, open, unjaded. But in this context, the disciples are elbowing toward the front, wondering "Who will be the greatest in the kingdom?" So Jesus points to someone who is small, seemingly insignificant, somebody not caught up in rank and title, someone unconcerned with status and privilege—and suggests that we must have such a mind, such a heart, or we will miss the kingdom, where everything seems turned upside down.

The world preaches "Get ahead! Look out for #1! More is better." But Jesus says "Get down. Be humble. Look out for little ones. Less is more." After all, why did God come down as a child instead of a giant?

*Prayer:* Lord, I want to remove myself from the competition to get ahead. Show me the child in me and in others.

## *Ninety-nine Sheep*

*Read Matthew 18:10-14*

**The Son of Man came to save the lost.**
*—Matthew 18:11*

The church is the only club whose reason to exist is for those who don't belong. We always pay attention to who isn't there, to whoever feels left out—who's been hurt by religion. We don't fret over the ninety-nine in the fold, while searching relentlessly for the one—and it's always just one, one at a time, just one.

Even within the church: we do not give preference to the tall, rich, strong, or good-looking. We don't even give preference to the stalwart volunteer or the time-tested leader. No, "the parts of the body which seem to be weaker are indispensable, and those parts of the body which we think less honorable we invest with the greater honor" (1 Corinthians 12:22). We do not pity the weak or those who struggle: we honor them; we are grateful for them. They remind us of our true selves before God and of Jesus, whose power is perfected in weakness (2 Corinthians 12:9).

*Prayer:* Lord, who is the one you want me to search for? Help me find that one and love it back home.

## *Church Discipline*

*Read Matthew 18:15-35*

***If your brother sins against you, go and tell him . . . between you and him alone.—Matthew 18:15***

Anticipating that Christians would struggle to get along with each other, Jesus mercifully laid out provision for how to deal with conflict. His first principle? Deal with conflict! We avoid conflict, and especially in church. But failing to talk to someone with whom you have a problem is not of God. Love the other person enough, and see that person as loved so powerfully by God that you cannot pretend, you cannot just let resentment fester, and you certainly can't gossip. Go, share, listen—and reconcile.

Jesus' counsel also suggests that there is such a thing as unacceptable behavior within church life. People act their worst, assuming anything goes at church—or else we nitpick over trivialities (like how someone is dressed or whether the flowers were arranged properly), instead of dealing with hurtful actions or theological craziness.

It's all about forgiveness—not seven times, but seventy times seven!

*Prayer:* Lord, teach me to deal with conflict. Press us into the hard but joyful labor of forgiveness.

## *Divorce*

*Read Matthew 19:1-15*

**What therefore God has joined together, let not man put asunder.** —*Matthew 19:6*

Is divorce permitted by Scripture? by God? Divorce has become common. It feels like individual failure, but the truth is we live in a culture of divorce; each new divorce is swept up in its tide. Society says "Life is about me and my fulfillment," and so we ask "Is divorce psychologically healthy? financially feasible?" What if we asked "How can we be faithful and serve God?"

Jesus said husband and wife are "one flesh." In his mercy, Jesus would plead with us: "Being joined physically is not trivial. It is a lifetime, irrevocable bond. I tell you this not to spoil the fun, but so you may not fritter yourself away, so you might know true joy."

Is divorce sin? How could it not be? Is divorce forgivable? Of course. How merciful Jesus was to people with fractured pasts!— including divorce (John 4:7-42); can Christians be as merciful when their friends are devastated by a broken home?

*Prayer:* Lord, deliver us from this society; we pray for those married and divorced.

31

## Mother's Dream

*Read Matthew 20:17-28*

**Whoever would be great among you must be your servant.** —*Matthew 20:26*

Ask any parent: "What is your dream for your child?" "I want my child to be happy" or "to fit in" or "to be financially independent."

The mother of James and John, proudly watching her sons, advocates that they should be perched in the most prominent positions in the kingdom. How off the mark is her understanding of Jesus' mission! His glory is suffering, not upward mobility but downward servanthood. Does she really want them near Jesus? for it will cost them ridicule—and even their lives. But if we love, we want those we love to love this Jesus, not some fantasy we attach to Jesus.

What is your dream? Perhaps not to be "happy" but to be "faithful," not to fit in but to be odd in a world that covets what is foolish, never independent but dependent upon God, never to be served but only to serve?

*Prayer:* Lord, chart your course for my life (and for those I love), not to scale up the world's ladder but to be like Jesus.

SATURDAY, MARCH 8, 2008

## *Cleansing the Temple*

*Read Matthew 21:12-17*

**Jesus entered the temple of God and drove out all
who sold and bought in the temple.**
**—Matthew 21:12**

Why did they kill Jesus? Storming into the
sacred precincts, flying into a rage instead of rev-
erently bowing, wrecking the place, and shout-
ing harsh judgment on the pious was reason
enough! "Maniacs" like Jesus weren't tolerated.

But what offended him? Were the dealers
crooked? the priests corrupt? Was it the mental-
ity that "everything is for sale"? Hadn't they
turned the Temple into the end, instead of the
*means* to the end? The Temple was to be "a house
of prayer" (Jesus quotes Isaiah 56:7), a window to
God, an altar where you sacrificed what was most
precious, a haven for healing—but the machin-
ery of running the place drowned out the mood
of prayer, sacrifice, and healing.

By rampaging through the Temple (and then
healing!), Jesus declared that no temple will be
required after his crucifixion. Jesus is the house
of prayer, the true means to life with God.

*Prayer:* Lord, rage through my routine,
through my church; purge it of what is fake
and be our holy temple.

## Render to Caesar

*Read Matthew 22:15-22*

**Render therefore to Caesar the things that are Caesar's, and to God the things that are God's.**
**—Matthew 22:21**

Stunned silence: those who tried to trap Jesus had no answer for his brilliant wisdom. They deceivingly flattered him, then popped the impossible question: does God permit the paying of taxes to Caesar or not? An annual property tax, a denarius, had to be paid. Jews resented the levy, plus the coins bore the blasphemous image of Caesar, claiming he was a god. If Jesus said yes, he's in league with Rome and the tax collectors; if no, he's siding with militant revolutionaries.

"Render to Caesar what is Caesar's." Jesus isn't legislating the separation of church and state. To Jesus, what belongs to Caesar is relatively trivial and temporary. What belongs to God is . . . everything! Followers of Jesus can be good citizens, but when loyalty to Jesus clashes with the realm of political reality, Jesus trumps. Give to God what belongs to God.

*Prayer:* Lord, remind me to think about whose image is on money, and then focus my zeal on what belongs to you.

## Married in Heaven?

*Read Matthew 22:23-33*

**In the resurrection they neither marry nor are given in marriage.** —*Matthew 22:30*

Pretending to seek instruction from Jesus, the Sadducees (who didn't believe there would be a resurrection at the end of time) think they will embarrass Jesus by asking: What if a woman were widowed seven times within a large family? Whose wife would she be in heaven?

Their error is one many Christians make today: thinking that heaven is this life as we know it prolonged forever—playing golf, eating chocolate éclairs, reuniting with those we know. But for Jesus, the resurrection is far more profound than this life. We are transformed; earthly limitations don't apply. No one belongs to anybody else; everyone will be "lost in wonder, love, and praise."

Jesus never underestimates the power of God, which solves all difficulties. Heaven will not be plagued with problems; and whatever is the most fantastic good we can imagine, heaven will be so much better as to put the good we think is good entirely in the shade.

*Prayer:* Lord, we are awed by your power and eagerly anticipate the resurrection.

*Greatest Commandment*

*Read Matthew 22:34-40*

**On these two commandments depend all the law and the prophets.** —*Matthew 22:40*

The Pharisees join the attack on Jesus, asking, "What is the greatest commandment?" Jesus, with words that would strike any Jew as beautifully true, cites from Deuteronomy 6:5—part of the Shema, which Jews recited every morning and evening. "You shall love the Lord your God with all your heart, soul, and might"

How odd: you *shall* love! Love isn't a feeling or a mood. Love is a commitment, a decision. Love can be commanded—and God demands no less than love from us!

Instead of giving a single answer, Jesus clasps a second to the first—not second in importance, but the two being of equal rank, like two sides to a coin or two banks to a river. "You shall love your neighbor as yourself" (Leviticus 19:18). If we love God, we love others; when we love others, we love God—we love the image of God in other people.

*Prayer:* Lord, we know that everything hangs on love of you and love of others. I want my entire life to hang on these and nothing else.

## Woe!

*Read Matthew 23:23-28*

**Woe to you, scribes and Pharisees, hypocrites! for you are like whitewashed tombs.**
**—Matthew 23:27**

Jesus unleashes a ferocious tirade against– not the crooks, the lazy or immoral—but the scribes and Pharisees, so zealous in their devotion to God they tithe even the seasonings in their food! They strain wine as they pour it on the off chance some microscopic organism might be ingested (violating Leviticus 11:41).

They are not wrong to strive for holiness in even the smallest matters. Jesus was no slacker and actually heightened the standard of how careful we should be to strive for God's will constantly. But, obsessed as they are with the minutiae, they miss the larger heart of the faith: What does the Lord require? Justice, mercy, and walking humbly before God (from Micah 6:8).

Devotion to God is not merely about picayune externals. How often does faith become something pasted on the outside of an otherwise unchanged life?

*Prayer:* Lord, forgive my superficial faith. I want to be clean and alive on the inside and the outside.

## O Jerusalem

*Read Matthew 23:37-39*

**How often would I have gathered your children together as a hen gathers her brood under her wings.** *—Matthew 23:37*

Pilgrims would travel in caravans, singing psalms, heady with the excitement of coming to the splendid city of God.

Jesus looks at Jerusalem and weeps—but not for joy. He understands the way God's holy city has puffed itself up, becoming a self-preserving fortress instead of a haven for the lost. Jesus is well aware that this city, which should welcome him as its Messiah, will reject his love. By the time Matthew wrote his Gospel, Jerusalem indeed was "forsaken and desolate": the Romans, crushing a Jewish revolt, destroyed the city in the year 70 A.D.

But instead of hurling thunderbolts at the city, Jesus tenderly imagines himself as a hen gathering her chicks—and his words are moving, not just because he devised a feminine image for God's love, but also because of the simple warmth and intimacy of vulnerable creatures, huddled in love.

*Prayer:* Lord, I imagine ways you weep over my life and over the church. Gather me, and gather your church, under your wings.

## Wars and Rumors of Wars

*Read Matthew 24:3-13*

**He who endures to the end will be saved.**
**—Matthew 24:13**

How did Jesus spend his last week? He reflected with his disciples—not about what happened in the past, but what would happen in the future. Standing on the Mount of Olives, a location associated in biblical prophecy with the end times, Jesus warned of dire sufferings to come in the waning hours of history.

The problem is not that religion will vanish from the earth. Instead, bogus religion will become fashionable; trivial spiritualities will vaunt themselves as the true way. We certainly see this in our day.

Following Jesus isn't about being sheltered from dark times; faith is about "enduring." Why endure? and how? The agony we face is akin to the birth pangs a mother endures. She is racked with pain; she can barely cope: but in the end there is new life, tender love, a bright future.

*Prayer:* Lord, give me strength to endure; keep my eyes on your future.

## Left Behind

*Read Matthew 24:36-51*

**Two women will be grinding at the mill; one is taken and one is left.**  —*Matthew 24:41*

The prospect of sudden disappearances delights some Christians, but planes crashing or children left desolate (as described in the bestselling *Left Behind* novels) should give us pause and grief.

Consider how much time has been spent, ink spilled, religious energy expended on calculating the timing of the end—when Jesus confessed that *even he* did not know! Jesus simply said to be prepared for it to happen before you finish this devotional—yet also to live as if we've got another million years down here. It's both. If you would live differently if Jesus were coming this evening, then change now. We will be judged by how we live, not by how clever our prognostications or understanding of timetables will have been.

*Prayer:* Lord, I want to be ready for your coming; my focus will be on living for you, if I have one more minute or if the end is long after I am deceased.

## Maidens and Lamps

*Read Matthew 25:1-13*

**Watch therefore, for you know neither the day nor the hour.** —Matthew 25:13

Imagine: young women, relatives and friends of a betrothed couple, walking out into the dark to welcome the groom. A parable of Palm Sunday, with torches instead of palm branches! The celebration is poised to begin. But with long working hours for the man in the fields and unanticipated holdups—when would he arrive?

In Jesus' parable, half are foolish, unprepared for a long wait. Half are wise, prepared for the long haul. So how are believers like these bridesmaids when it comes to looking for the kingdom of God?

Even the foolish bridesmaids were eager for the groom to come; however, they expected the groom to come when they were ready, not when he was ready. They forced their own preferred timetable—only to miss his coming. Who knew Jesus was coming on Palm Sunday?

*Prayer:* Lord, I want to be ready for you and prepared to wait until you are ready to come. I will get on your timetable; I will pray, do good, and wait for you to act.

41

## Talents

*Read Matthew 25:14-30*

**Well done, good and faithful servant.**
**—Matthew 25:21**

"Talents" is an unfortunate translation of the Greek *talanta*. A "talent" isn't a special ability I have, my passion in life. *Talanton* is "a bucketful of gold." Just one *talanta*, which weighted seventy pounds, would stagger any recipient; you'd have no idea what to do with it.

Jesus (who would never have seen that kind of money) used an outlandish image: the gospel is like winning five lotteries. Isn't Jesus suggesting that an astonishingly ravishing gift has been unloaded upon an unsuspecting church; and we are to offer up, not our individual abilities, but the frank admission of our *in*ability to handle it?

We populate church committees with the best people who confidently offer insights from their experience. But maybe God needs people who will huddle up, shake their heads, and confess, "We just have no idea; the treasure is too big, too heavy." Maybe then we can dare something for God.

*Prayer:* Lord, the gospel is too huge, too precious; you use it, despite my inability.

## Sheep and Goats

*Read Matthew 25:31-46*

**As you did it to one of the least of these my brethren, you did it to me.** *—Matthew 25:40*

Collecting food, participating in clothing drives, visiting the sick: familiar, commendable activities. What is stunning about Jesus' last sermon is his suggestion that your salvation depends upon whether you do these things or not. Serving the poor isn't an optional, experience to make you feel good about yourself. How stark the choice: whether you discover the kingdom or plummet into eternal punishment, depends on whether you were a servant or not.

Aren't we saved by grace, not works (Ephesians 2:8)? But faith without works is dead (James 2:17).

Mother Teresa, whose life was an embodied sermon on Matthew 25:31-46, wrote, "At the end of life we . . . will be judged by, I was hungry and you gave me to eat, I was naked and you clothed me, I was homeless and you took me in."

*Prayer:* Lord, forgive my sins of omission. I promise to look for you among the poor.

## Peter's Denial

*Read Matthew 26:69-75*

***[Peter] denied it with an oath, "I do not know the
man."***                         ***—Matthew 26:72***

Peter was supposed to be the "rock"
(Matthew 16:18) on which Jesus would build
the church! But when the pressure rose, Peter
became crumbling sandstone. He'd been the
first to confess Jesus as "the Christ, the Son of
the living God" (Matthew 16:16); now he is
the first to lie and fake. Peter swore "Even if all
fall away on account of you, I never will"
(26:33 NIV); how swiftly he was unmasked as
phony! No one in authority threatened him
with death! Peter simply was chillingly embarrassed by the mere association with Jesus.

Peter's denial wasn't a momentary slip of
the tongue; he is adamant, three times swear-
ing he never knew Jesus. Thankfully, even
though Jesus anticipated and predicted
Peter's weakness (Matthew 26:34), Jesus did
not give up on him and used him to be the
rock in spite of himself.

*Prayer:* Lord, I shudder to think how flimsy my
faith would be in the face of real danger. Have
mercy on me and use me in spite of myself.

## This Is My Body

*Read Matthew 26:17-30*

***Take, eat; this is my body.***     *—Matthew 26:26*

Jesus had this striking habit of making an issue out of meals, offending against custom, one *faux pas* after another. He ate with tax collectors and was accused of gluttony; he rudely urged his hosts not to invite their friends or the "right" people, but rather the poor, maimed, and blind; Jesus permitted an unseemly woman to wash his feet with her hair; he washed the feet of his disciples. When we think of this sacrament, we need to recall the way Jesus conducted himself at table.

The Lord's Supper is a thanksgiving (Acts 2:46), a fellowship meal (1 Corinthians 10:16-17), a memorial (Luke 22:19), even a sacrifice (Hebrews 9:14). Ignatius called it "the medicine of immortality," for this meal anticipates the glorious banquet that heaven will be. The Lord's supper is based on an invitation that is "as open as the outstretched arms of Christ on the cross."

*Prayer:* Lord, we accept your invitation to your table.

## Forsaken

*Read Matthew 27:45-50*

***My God, my God, why hast thou forsaken me?***
***—Matthew 27:46***

The God who said, "Let there be light" (Genesis 1:3), the God in whom there is no darkness at all" (1 John 1:5) was so grieved over the suffering of his beloved Son that the sky grew dark mid-afternoon. The crucifixion is so familiar that we may forget the brutal, gruesome horror—and how shockingly unexpected that such a moment is the wide-open door into the heart of God.

Jesus, gasping for breath, cried out: "My God, my God, why have you forsaken me?" Just as his mother had taught him, Jesus prayed Scripture: the twenty-second Psalm.

Had God forsaken Jesus? Might God forsake me? Doesn't Jesus' cry leave us space to cry out in the darkness when we seem forsaken by God? God did not remain aloof in heaven, but entered into human suffering. So in every kind of darkness—whatever we have faced or will face, even in the hour of our own death—Jesus cries out with us.

*Prayer:* Lord, with all my heart I thank you for the love of Jesus poured out on all of us.

## Judas's "Repentance"

*Read Matthew 27:1-10*

**[Judas] repented and brought back the thirty pieces of silver.** —*Matthew 27:3*

Matthew, more than the other Gospels, has a special interest in Judas. Judas betrayed Jesus for money—but then he "repented." Fascinating: he was sorry, full of regret—but was it genuine repentance?

Describing Judas's remorse, Matthew uses the Greek word *metamelomai*, which is different from the word usually translated "repent"—*metanoeo*. Judas's stricken mood of *metamelomai* is one of guilt, immense regret, dark desperation. But this is not what God asks of us. Peter denies Jesus, but Peter repents (*metanoeo*). He is guilty, but reaches out for forgiveness; he feels not despair but hope.

How self-centered is Judas's *metamelomai* repentance! It's all about me; it's all on me. Left to his own devices, Judas, focused on nothing but himself, feels no option but death. But the joy of *metanoeo* repentance is all about God; it's all about his mercy; he's the success; he births new life.

*Prayer:* Lord, move me beyond guilt and remorse and toward healing and new life.

47

## Great Commission

*Read Matthew 28:11-20*

**I am with you always.** —*Matthew 28:20*

Easter dawns; Jesus continues teaching. Matthew's Gospel began with the angel announcing a sacred name: Emmanuel, God with us (Matthew 1:23). As if to form bookends—or better, strong loving arms enfolding us in a powerfully tender embrace—Matthew ends with Jesus making the only promise that matters: I will be with you.

No greater comfort envelops us; no more provocative challenge prods us. Jesus' presence is deeper and more lasting than any we could ever know.

No surprise, then, that Jesus catapults the disciples (and us) into the world to reach others, loving the unlovable, corralling those nobody else wants, living a life that is compelling, good, at peace. The Christian never vacations from "going into all the world."

*Prayer:* Lord, we will be your missionaries, not because we have to but because we are so engrossed in the wonder of you that we cannot be anything else, teaching by our lives, passionate to grab a hand and say, "He's the One; he is Emmanuel."